seeking religion

The **Jewish** Experience

Liz Aylett and Kevin O'Donnell

Hodder & Stoughton

A MEMBER OF THE HODDER HEADLINE GROUP

Acknowledgements

The Publishers would like to thank the following for permission to reproduce material in this volume:

BBC for the quote by Nathan Sharansky from *When I Get To Heaven*, 1987 and the quote by Julia Neuberger from *Open Space*; BBC/The Chief Rabbi for the extract from the broadcast by the Chief Rabbi, Radio 3, Eve of Rosh Hashanah, September 1987; Channel 4 for the quote by Gerson Cohen from *Heritage Conversation*, January 1988; HarperCollins for the extracts from *This is My God* by Herman Wouk; *Jewish Chronicle* for the quotations by Ida Nudel, reproduced by permission, Penguin UK for the extracts from *The Diary of a Young Girl: The Definitive Edition* by Anne Frank, edited by Otto Frank and Mirjam Pressler, translated by Susan Massotty (Viking, 1997) copyright © The Anne Frank-Fonds, Basle, Switzerland, 1991. English translation copyright © Doubleday, a division of Bantam Doubleday Dell Publishing Group Inc, 1995. Reproduced by permission of Penguin Books Ltd.

Words in heavy print **like this** are explained in the glossary on page 62.

Orders: please contact Bookpoint Ltd, 39 Milton Park, Abingdon, Oxon OX14 4TD. Telephone: (44) 01235 400414, Fax: (44) 01235 400454. Lines are open from 9.00–6.00, Monday to Saturday, with a 24 hour message answering service. Email address: orders@bookpoint.co.uk

British Library Cataloguing in Publication Data
A catalogue record for this title is available from The British Library

ISBN 0 340 74773 0

First published 1991
Second edition 2000

Impression number	10	9	8	7	6	5	4	3	2	1
Year	2005	2004	2003	2002	2001	2000				

Cover photo from David Rose.
All illustrations supplied by Daedalus, with special thanks to John McIntyre.
Typeset by Wearset, Boldon, Tyne and Wear.
Printed for Hodder & Stoughton Educational, a division of Hodder Headline Plc, 338 Euston Road, London NW1 3BH by Printer Trento, Italy.

The Publishers would like to thank the following for their permission to reproduce copyright photographs in this book:

AKG Photo, London: p. 53; Ancient Art and Architecture Collection Ltd: p. 16; Associated Press Library: pp. 54, 56; CIRCA Photo Library (Barrie Searle): pp. 35, 40, 43, 44, 46, 52, 61; Corbis pp. 15, 20, 25, 32, 41, 48, 59; Hulton Getty: pp. 9, 21r; Life File: pp. 4, 14, 17, 19, 21l; Christine Osborne/MEP: pp. 8, 18, 26l, 28, 37, 47, 50, 55, 58; David Rose: pp. 7, 26r, 27, 29, 31, 36, 42, 49; Topham Picturepoint: pp. 22, 23.

Every effort has been made to contact the holders of copyright material but if any have been inadvertently overlooked, the Publisher will be pleased to make the necessary alterations at the first opportunity.

CE = Common Era
BCE = Before the Common Era
CE corresponds to AD, and BCE corresponds to BC. The years are the same, but CE and BCE can be used by anyone, regardless of their religion. (AD and BC are Christian: AD stands for Anno Domini – In the Year of our Lord; BC stands for Before Christ.)

Contents

3

Who are the Jews?

▲ *A modern Jewish family*

The above people are all Jews. Well-known Jews might be film makers (Steven Speilberg), TV personalities (Esther Rantzen), singers (Barbra Streisand) or scientists (Einstein). Jews live in many different countries of the world, and have done so for centuries. The map below shows the main places where Jewish communities can be found, and approximate numbers of inhabitants.

Many Jews live in Israel today. However, the nation of Israel has only existed since 1948. It was many centuries before this that the Jews lived in large numbers in this area. In the meantime, they dispersed throughout the nations, and small communities carried on in the Middle East, living alongside Arabs. The Jewish people originate from the Middle East.

A symbol for the Jewish faith is the Star of David. King David was one of their ancient heroes.

▼ *Jewish people live in many countries throughout the world*

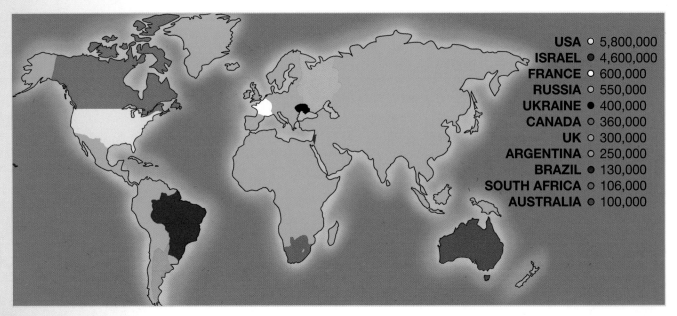

USA	○ 5,800,000
ISRAEL	◉ 4,600,000
FRANCE	○ 600,000
RUSSIA	○ 550,000
UKRAINE	● 400,000
CANADA	○ 360,000
UK	○ 300,000
ARGENTINA	○ 250,000
BRAZIL	● 130,000
SOUTH AFRICA	○ 106,000
AUSTRALIA	○ 100,000

▲ A 'Who am I?' of famous Jews

1 **a)** What gifts have the modern Jews in this chapter given to our lives?
  b) Think about a gift you have. Under a photo or drawing of yourself, write about this gift.
2 Choose two Jews from the past who have helped to make life better in some way.
  a) Write down what each of them did.
  b) Write down two words which you think describe each person.
  c) Describe what might have happened if those people had not lived.
3 **a)** Which country has the most Jews living in it, and which has the least?
  b) Which part of the world do the Jews originate from?
  c) Which country or locality do you regard as your homeland? Draw a simple map of it and write across this what you feel about your homeland.
4 Draw the Star of David symbol.

Do you know how many relations you have? Perhaps you belong to a small family. Or you may have many brothers, sisters, cousins, aunts, uncles. The list could go on and on. But none of your relations would have been born if it had not been for your great-grandparents. And many more – going back hundreds of years.

The Jewish people believe that they can trace their beginnings back to one person – a man called Abram. They call him the Father of the Jews. He lived nearly four thousand years ago, in the country now called Iraq.

◀ A ziggurat at Ur

Archaeologists have found the remains of the ancient city of Ur. The photograph shows one of their huge temples, a **ziggurat,** where the sun and the moon were worshipped as gods.

Most people at that time **worshipped** many gods, but Abram came to believe there was just one true God. He taught his family that this God cared for them. So they should worship only Him.

When Abram was old, God told him to leave his home and travel to a new country. God promised that He would give Abram this land and that his **descendants** would become a great nation. In return, Abram and all his family were to obey and worship Him.

▼ A map of the Middle East in Abraham's time. He was born in Ur and moved to Haran when he was young

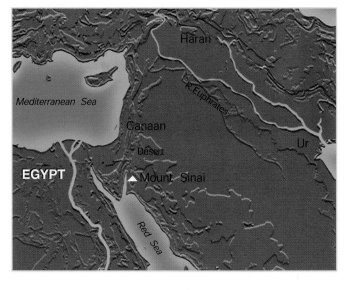

Abram was puzzled. He had no children. How could he have any descendants now? However, he trusted God. So he and his wife, Sarai, set off towards Canaan. His nephew's family went too.

The whole family settled in Canaan and were known as Hebrews. This comes from a word meaning 'from the other side', because they came from the other side of the River Euphrates. They did not forget their promise to worship God.

And then Sarai had a son in her old age. They were amazed. They called the boy Isaac, which means 'laughter'. Abram was given a new name, Abraham, 'father of the people'.

Sarai laughed because she did not believe she would actually have a child, and when she did, she was overjoyed. She was then called Sarah.

Abraham thought it was his religious duty to sacrifice Isaac, his firstborn son. Sadly, this was a common custom at the time of offering something precious back to the gods. The Bible says that God sent an angel to stop him. Abraham then sacrificed a ram, instead.

◀ God tested Abraham by ordering him to sacrifice Isaac. When Abraham was ready to do this, God sent an angel to stop him. Abraham sacrificed a ram instead

1 Make up a travel diary that Abraham might have written about his journeys.

2 a) Write down the meanings of the names Abraham and Isaac.
   b) Why was Isaac given this name?
   c) Find out the meaning of your own name.

3 Abraham was called a Hebrew. Why?

4 Which of the following words do you think describe Abraham? Give a reason for each choice.
   brave; foolish; old; obedient; cruel; friendly; trusting; bloodthirsty.

5 Read Genesis 22: 1–14. Abraham was willing to offer his son in sacrifice.
   a) How did God show Abraham that he did not want such cruel offerings?
   b) Write about something very important to you that you would only give up if you had to.

Many years after Abraham's death, there was **famine** in Canaan. The Hebrews moved to Egypt, where there was plenty of food. At first, everything went well. But later the Egyptians used them as slaves to build two great new cities.

Later, the Hebrews became known as the Israelites after one of their ancestors called Israel (Prince of God). Their great leader was Moses. He asked the Pharaoh of Egypt to set the slaves free. The Pharaoh refused; slaves were useful. At last, however, God sent ten horrible **plagues** and the Pharaoh finally let the Israelites go.

They escaped into the desert, an event known as the Exodus. There, they lived for forty years, while trying to return to Canaan. Moses died during this time. So a man called Joshua led them back into the land God had promised to them.

The people were divided into twelve tribes and the land was shared between them. Each tribe was named after one of Abraham's great-grandsons. The name 'Jew' comes from the tribe of Judah.

The Book of Exodus describes the ten plagues that followed each other, causing destruction in Egypt until the Pharaoh let the Hebrews go. These fit very closely with the conditions of severe drought and freak weather conditions – low water in the Nile turns red, cloudy and polluted (like blood); frogs come onto dry land; infection and insects abound with the lack of water; storms and darkness occur as the weather starts to change; locusts seek out food where they can; disease spreads and kills off many ('the firstborn'). The point is that Moses felt called by God to set his people free just when these disasters were striking. Was the miracle in the timing?

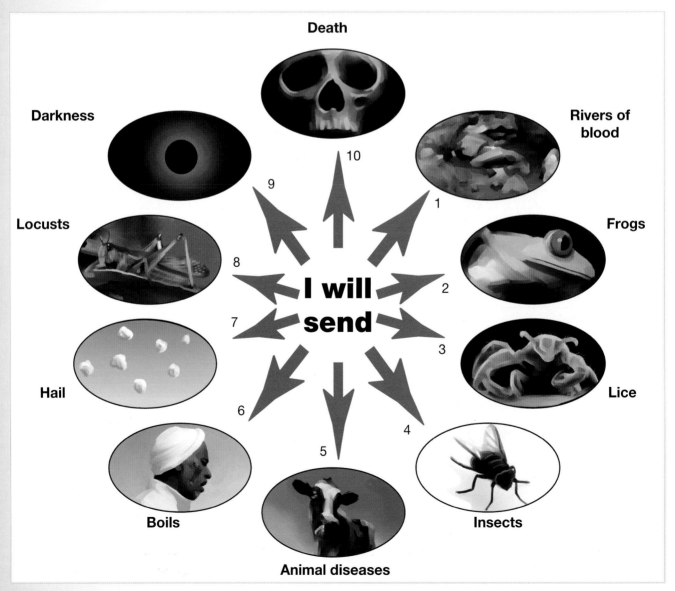

Death

Darkness

Rivers of blood

Locusts

Frogs

10

9

1

I will send

8

2

7

3

Hail

Lice

6

4

5

Boils

Insects

Animal diseases

▲ *The ten plagues which struck the Egyptians. See how each is more horrible than the one before*

◄ *African slaves waiting to be sold*

The ancient Israelites were unique among all the nations of the ancient world. Only they told a story that their ancestors had been slaves. Other people would have tried to forget this and would have invented a more glorious beginning. Many nations claimed that they had descended from a great hero, a warrior, a king, or a god. The Romans said they came from the two children of the war god, Mars. The Jews said they came from the slaves in Egypt. This honesty suggests that the story is based upon truth. The events of the Exodus were told and retold, down the generations, as *the* event that started the Jewish faith.

Centuries later, other slaves were to hear the story of the Exodus, of Moses and the plagues, and they took comfort from them. When African slaves were taken across the sea to the USA, and the Caribbean, they heard about the Bible. Right at the start of this holy book was a story about escaped slaves, slaves helped by God! They told their own stories about Moses and sang their own songs about him. These are known as Negro Spirituals, and music such as the Blues and Jazz came from this style. A famous singer of Spirituals was Paul Robeson.

1 What was the Exodus?

2 **a)** How do modern scholars explain the Ten Plagues?

  b) Do you think this helps people to believe the Bible story, or does it take something away?

  c) 'The miracle might have been in the timing.' What does this mean?

3 **a)** How did many ancient people describe where their tribe or nation had come from?

  b) What was different about the ideas of the Jews?

  c) Why did African slaves sing songs about Moses, years later?

4 Make up an imaginary tribe that you would like to belong to. Then

  a) Write an origin story, claiming to have come from something great.

  b) Write a different story, claiming to have been helped by someone great when your people were in serious trouble.

5 Hebrew, Israelite, Jew – different names for the same race, at different times. Where did each name come from?

◀ *Joseph dreamed of seven fat cows and seven thin ones. This was a warning about the future*

Judaism has many ancient heroes, such as Abraham and Moses, and their stories are in the early parts of the Bible. The story of Joseph, a descendent of Abraham, is told in the Book of Genesis.

Joseph's brothers were jealous of him – he was their father's favourite. They pushed him down a well, but some slave traders took him away and sold him in Egypt. There, he worked hard until a woman tried to trick him, and he was put in prison. He had an ability to interpret dreams, and he was the only person in the land who could make sense of Pharaoh's dreams of seven fat and seven thin cows, with seven good sheaves of corn, and seven poor ones.

Joseph warned Pharaoh that after seven good years of large harvests would come seven years of famine. The Egyptians prepared to store all the extra grain. Joseph was rewarded and became Pharaoh's chief official.

During a time of famine, the Hebrews came into Egypt looking for food. Joseph recognised his brothers and made peace with them. The Hebrews were allowed to settle. It was many years later that new Pharaohs who came to power turned against the Hebrews and made them into slaves. That is why Moses had to help to set them free.

1 Why do you think Abraham, Joseph and Moses were great heroes to the ancient Hebrews? Write a sentence for each one.

2 a) Talk, as a class, about modern-day heroes. Why are these people heroes?

b) Who is one of your heroes? Write a few lines about this person, and stick a picture of him or her into your book.

c) Design an imaginary hero who would tackle one of the world's problems.

3 Read about Pharaoh's dreams in Genesis 41.

a) Draw your own pictures of these, and explain what they meant.

b) Have you ever had a dream that warned you of something, or seemed to come true?

You may belong to a club or society. There is probably a set of rules for all the members. The rules will have been drawn up by members of the club, maybe many years ago. Often, the rules are written down in a book.

We might have our own rules that we try to follow, our code for living, such as the Golden Rule – treat others as you want them to treat you. Human rights, care for animals, and care for the Earth, are all a part of a code for living.

The Jews have special books, in which they can read all the rules of their religion. The oldest of these is the Bible, the Tenach. This is really a collection of twenty-four books. (Christians call them the Old Testament.)

For Jews, the most important part of the Tenach is the first five books. These are called the Torah. It means teaching. The Torah is a mixture of stories and **commandments**. It describes the **creation** of the world and the early history of the Jews, ending with the death of Moses.

In Exodus chapter 19 we read that God called Moses to the top of a mountain. God told Moses that He had chosen the Israelites as His special people. He repeated the promise made to Abraham, that He would look after them and lead them to a new land.

In return they had to keep God's commandments and to set a good example to all people. Moses was given two stone tablets with the most important rules written on them. These are the Ten Commandments.

The Hebrews had been set free from slavery. Now they were to follow God's laws out of gratitude.

▲ *Slogans such as these remind us of how we should behave*

BAN CRUELTY TO ANIMALS

STOP RACISM

TREAT ME AS YOU WOULD LIKE TO BE TREATED

▼ *Thank you! The Hebrews were set free by Moses, and they followed the Commandments out of gratitude*

There are 613 commandments in the Torah! Many of them deal with the Temple sacrifices. Today there is no Temple; there are no sacrifices. So those laws no longer apply. But the others teach Jews what they should do in just about every part of their lives. For this Jewish lady, the Torah is much more than a book:

> ● The commandments in the Torah are my guide to living. The stories in the Torah really happened, the people in the Torah are real people that I can identify with.
>
> I firmly believe in the Torah as a complete way of life. I don't consider it to be a holy way of life. It is simply my way of life.

Another holy book is called the Talmud. It means study. It gives advice from early Jewish leaders who studied the Torah. They worked out rules to help Jews to keep the commandments.

▲ *Which of the Ten Commandments are pictured here?*

1 Match the words on the left to their meaning:

The Torah	study of the Torah
The Tenach	teaching
The Talmud	book which tells the story of Moses
Exodus	the Jewish Bible

2 Find the Ten Commandments in Exodus 20.

a) Make three columns on a page.

(i) In the left-hand one write the numbers 1–10, one for each Commandment.

(ii) Look at the drawings on this page and decide which drawing fits which Commandment. Put the letter of the drawing in the second column, next to the correct number.

(iii) In the third column write *yes* if the person in the drawing is obeying the Commandment, and *no* if they are not.

b) The last five Commandments begin with 'do not'. Rewrite each one so that it starts with 'Always'. For example, number eight might become: 'Always leave other people's belongings alone.'

c) Pick any one Commandment. Give reasons why you think it is important today.

3 a) In groups, make up a Code for Living that you think would be good for everyone to follow.

b) Work out two or three rules which will show people how to keep each of your commandments.

● Prophets

Many books in the Hebrew Bible are about the prophets. A prophet was a messenger who believed that God had spoken to him. Some things were about the future, but most things were for the people then. God's prophets were brave men who would challenge evil kings and appeal to their consciences. One famous prophet was Elijah, and he challenged King Ahab, who stopped worshipping the one God and worshipped idols instead. When it had not rained for weeks, Elijah issued a challenge to the king. The priests of his gods should build an altar and put a sacrifice on it. Then they should call upon their gods and see if fire fell from heaven. They tried, and nothing happened. Elijah built an altar, and fire fell when he prayed. The 'fire from heaven' would have been lightning, and this would have also signalled the end of the drought. Was it an amazing coincidence that it struck only Elijah's sacrifice, or was it guided by God?

Another prophet challenged King David. David had had an affair with someone else's wife, and he had sent her husband into a battle, hoping he would be killed. He was. The prophet Nathan visited the king and told him a story.

▲ The prophet Nathan visits King David

● Songs and Sayings

One famous section of the Hebrew Bible is the Book of Psalms. These are songs based upon praise poems or prayers. They are very honest and open, expressing anger and doubt as well as faith in God. They have been compared to singing the Blues, and Jews have recited Psalms of anger or doubt at difficult times, such as these verses from Psalm 22:

> ● My God, my God, why have you forsaken me?
> Why are you so far from helping me, from the words of my groaning?
> O my God, I cry by day, but you do not answer; and by night, but find no rest.

Other Psalms are full of peace and praise, such as Psalm 23:

> ● The Lord is my shepherd, I shall not want.
> He makes me lie down in green pastures;
> he leads me beside still waters;
> he restores my soul . . .

The Psalms repeat the same feeling or idea, doubling up the lines to make an impact – shepherd/led to green pastures; led by still waters/soul restored.

The Book of Proverbs contains many wise sayings.

> ● Wine is a mocker, strong drink a brawler, and whoever is led astray by it is not wise.
>
> ● It is honourable to refrain from strife, but every fool is quick to quarrel.
>
> ● A soft answer turns away wrath, but a harsh word stirs up anger.
>
> ● Happy are those who find wisdom, and those who get understanding, for her income is better than silver, and her revenue better than gold.

1 a) What was a prophet?
  b) What contest did Elijah hold, and what happened when he prayed?
  c) How might the 'fire from heaven' be explained?
  d) What story did Nathan tell to King David, and why did it apply to him?
2 Try to write a Psalm about something bad in life, and then something good. Try to use the same style, using two lines at a time that say the same thing in different ways.
3 In groups, choose one of the Proverbs and act out a rôle-play based upon it.

▶ *Beside still waters*

● One God

The Jewish belief about God can be put very simply. There is only one God. He created the world and He sees and knows everything.

God gave them His laws for two reasons. First, so that they would know how to worship Him. Second, so that they would be able to show other people how to live in a kind and caring way. Jews believe that this relationship with God will continue only so long as they remain faithful to Judaism.

The idea that there is only one God has a special name. It is called **monotheism**. The first Hebrew which a Jewish child learns is a prayer called the Shema. This is part of the Torah, and the first words sum up the belief in one God.

> ● I used to wonder whether a man could really call to mind and recite the Creed (Shema). Then once, during a **typhoon** in the Pacific, I was almost blown off the deck of a ship. I remember quite clearly thinking, as I went sliding towards my fate, 'Well, if I drown, let me say the Shema as I go'.
>
> Herman Wouk: *This is my God*

Jews believe that God watches over the world and cares for all the people in it. Jews try to follow God's example. One way to do this is to treat other people as we should like them to treat us. The Torah says:

> ● Do not take revenge on anyone or continue to hate him, but love your neighbour as you love yourself.
>
> ● Do not hold back the wages of someone you have hired, not even for one night.
>
> ● Do not cheat when you use weights and measures.
>
> ● If a fellow Israelite's donkey or cow has fallen down, don't ignore it, help him to get the animal to its feet again.

Shema Yisrael, Adonai Elohenu, Adonai Echad.

Hear, O Israel, the Lord our God, the Lord is one.

▲ *The text of the Shema in Hebrew and English*

The Shema should also be the last thing a Jew says before death. The American playwright Herman Wouk's experience shows that this is not as unlikely as it may sound.

▲ *Young Jewish children learning the Shema*

● The Messiah

Sadly, people do not always think about others. But Jews look forward to the coming of the Messiah, God's messenger of peace. Then everyone will obey God's commandments. When this happens, the whole world will be at peace.

Christians believe that Jesus was the Messiah. But Jews look at the world today and say that they are still waiting. They are waiting for a human being who will be so special that he will bring everyone together.

One Rabbi heard that the Messiah had come. He looked out of his window and saw a dog chasing a cat. 'No he hasn't. The world has not changed!' he replied.

There are different ideas of what the Messiah might be like, and some Jews see this as a spiritual force that will improve the world, rather than one special man.

All through history, there have been people claiming to be the Messiah – men of peace like Jesus, and men of war who rose up to fight the Romans or some other **foe**.

The Counterfeit Meſſiah of the Iews at smyrna 1666 Page.

▶ *This is Shabbetai Zevi. He claimed to be the Messiah. The people welcomed him. Later they realised his claim was false*

16

1 Copy out these sentences, using the correct word or words from the brackets:
   a) The Jews believe in (one God/many gods).
   b) The Jewish people were (punished/chosen) to set a good example to others.
   c) The first prayer a Jewish child learns is the (Torah/Shema).
2 Copy out the Hebrew words of the Shema and say what this means in English.
3 **a)** Write a paragraph about someone you know of who tries to treat others as they would like to be treated.
   b) Write a few lines about a time when you have not done this.

   c) What do you think you should have done?
   d) Write down your own example of how to treat other people.
   e) Draw a picture of somebody following your example.
4 **a)** What do Jews believe the world will be like when the Messiah comes?
   b) Describe one thing that you would change in the world.
   c) Draw a scene from the world after the Messiah comes.

● The World to Come

Jews speak of Olam Ha'ba, 'the world to come'.

God has told Jews how to get the most out of their lives. But the end of life on Earth does not mean the end of everything. There will be another kind of life which lasts forever, although nobody knows what it will be like.

Some wonder if this is a heaven in a spiritual world, or a new Earth in a new universe, without death and disease.

Belief in an afterlife is an excellent reason for leading a good life on Earth. This belief is strong in most religions. A Jewish girl wrote:

> ● I believe that there is a Heaven. I think that once we die, we do go to Heaven. After reading the Torah it is obvious that G_d loves us too much to end our lives after we die.

You will notice that she does not write out all the letters of God's name. Jews believe that his name is holy. This means they must treat it with respect. Some Jews prefer not to write out the whole name. They feel it would insult God if the paper with his name on were torn or dropped.

In this book, we will write God in full. But remember that any Jewish pupils among you would like God's name to be treated carefully.

◀ Sunrise, a promise of light and new beginnings

1 a) What does 'Olam Ha'ba' mean?
  b) What might this be like?
  c) Why does the Jewish girl believe there must be a Heaven?
  d) Do you think that this life is all that there is?
2 a) Why is there a picture of a bright light in darkness, on this page?
  b) Design your own symbol for life after death.

▲ *Inside the synagogue, showing the* **bimah** *and the Ark*

Synagogue means assembly or gathering. The synagogue is the meeting place for Jews. It is where they pray, study, and talk. The building may be large or small, old or modern. It may be anywhere in the world. But certain things will be the same. You can see them in the picture above.

Jews do their best to go to the services on the Sabbath day, their holy day. It lasts from Friday evening to Saturday night. Orthodox men attend on Friday evening and then return home for the meal. Reform synagogues usually have later services so the whole family can go after they have eaten. Saturday morning services are for everybody.

Any member of the **congregation** can lead them through the order of service found in the **siddur**, the Jewish prayer-book. It does not have to be a rabbi. But in an Orthodox synagogue it is always a man. In a Reform synagogue, a woman or man may be the leader. Orthodox Jews are more traditional and strict.

Most synagogues, however, do have a rabbi. This is always a man in Orthodox synagogues but there are several women Reform rabbis. An Orthodox rabbi describes what happens in his synagogue.

- We have readings from the Psalms. We have special prayers and a reading from the Torah. During the morning service we go up, take out one of the scrolls, and take it up to the reader's desk. Then I will open up the scroll and read from it in Hebrew.

  At the end I hold up the scroll, and say a prayer in English for Her Majesty followed by a prayer for the State of Israel. Then we take the scroll down again and put it back into the Ark. The Ark is closed. After the service, we usually have a gathering of the congregation in the hall. We have **Kiddush** over wine and cakes

18

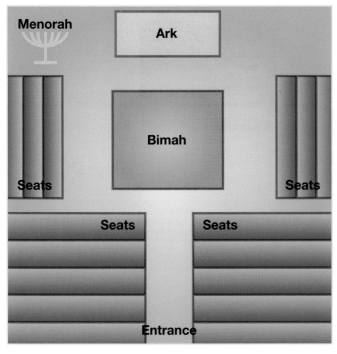

▲ *A plan of the synagogue*

The Torah, the Law of Moses, is a sacred text for Jews. The scrolls are kept in the Ark (meaning container), and they are carried out with great solemnity. The central part of the service is hearing these read aloud.

▲ *Lighting the menorah. This one has eight candles and is used at a special Jewish festival*

The Menorah – the seven-branched candlestick – reminds Jews of God and of creation. The light symbolises God's presence – holy, loving and true, and the number seven is a special number. It stands for perfection, and also reminds people of the story of the creation of the world in the Bible, where God created everything in seven days. However, many Jews do not take this literally. They feel that God created the world over a long period of time, in seven stages.

Everyone has something in their lives that is special, whether they are religious or not. What things in this bedroom are very special to the owner?

1 **a)** Draw each of the following objects in a synagogue: (i) the menorah; (ii) the Torah scrolls; (iii) the Commandments (Exodus 20: 3–17).
   b) For each one, explain why it is important.
2 Gather up the Codes for Living that the class designed earlier. In groups, create scrolls by sticking sheets of paper together. Write out parts of the Codes for Living upon the scrolls and display these.
3 Sit around a lit candle and focus on this. Go around the circle and find out what feelings and ideas this might suggest. List all the things that light might symbolise.
4 What is special to you? This might be a place, an object or a person. Write a few lines about this, and stick in some pictures.

In an Orthodox synagogue, nearly all the service is in Hebrew. Only the prayer for the Royal Family and the **sermon** are in English. In Reform synagogues there is more English, as a Reform rabbi explains.

> ● There is some English in our service. The main parts of the service, such as the Shema, would nearly always be in Hebrew. In my service, I try to have something like seventy-five per cent Hebrew, twenty-five per cent English.

WESTON ORTHODOX SYNAGOGUE
SABBATH SERVICES THIS WEEK
Friday 4.10pm • Saturday 9-11.45am
LADIES AND CHILDREN →
← MEN

EASTON REFORM SYNAGOGUE
SABBATH SERVICES
Fridays 8pm • Saturdays 11am-12.30pm
THIS WAY, EVERYBODY →

▲ *Differences between the Orthodox and Reform synagogues*

Jewish men should also pray every evening, morning and afternoon. The prayers can be held in the synagogue as long as there are at least ten males over the age of thirteen present.

Most people lead such busy lives that it is impossible to get to their synagogue as often as this. But they can pray anywhere. The important thing is that they really mean what they say.

Prayer is a way of talking to God. Sometimes people who are not religious think that praying just means asking God for something which they want, like a new bike or good exam results. But those are selfish prayers. When Jewish people pray, they:
● praise God for His creation
● ask Him to care for people in trouble
● thank Him for looking after everyone
● ask Him to forgive them for doing wrong
● pray for peace all over the world.

▲ *This synagogue is in South Africa*

1 Divide your page into two columns. Head one column *Orthodox* and the other *Reform*. Copy these statements into the correct column. (Careful: some statements may belong to both.) Pages 21–22 may help.
  a) I worship one God.
  b) My synagogue allows women rabbis.
  c) I don't sit with my husband in the synagogue.
  d) Our Sabbath Eve service starts at different times each week.
  e) Our whole family goes to the synagogue after the Sabbath meal.
2 Look at the five things Jews think about when they pray. Write a list of things which you are thankful for.
3 Find out where your nearest synagogue is. In groups, write a letter to the rabbi, asking if you may visit his or her synagogue. Then, as a class, pick the best letter and send it.

▲ *Party time in the new Millennium!*

▲ *A Jewish family in the 1880s*

The two photographs show people of today, and from Victorian times. Many things have changed since then. There are different customs, fashions and new technology. Life changes, and each age brings its own advances and problems. For example, our age has nuclear weapons and toxic waste. We go on learning more about science, and we can cure more diseases, or build new machinery. We would not think of following all the laws from the Victorian times, or even the Middle Ages, today! However, some old laws might still make sense, such as those that stop theft.

Religions have a great deal of thinking to do about their old laws, which are usually written in their holy books. How many of these should still be followed, and how many should be changed? The holy books were written a long time ago, when people did not understand so much about the world, and customs were different. Yet, if God inspired these writings, they might be true for all time. Religions have traditionalists, who want to keep everything unchanged, and modernists, who want to bring the faith up to date and make it easier to follow. The Jews have the same arguments, and there are Orthodox and Reform Jews, as we saw in the last chapter.

Some old laws might have been good for their time, but do they make sense now? The Torah forbids Jews to eat certain foods, such as pork or shellfish. Some Reform Jews think this is outdated as it was for reasons of hygiene – pork and shellfish go off very quickly without proper refrigeration. Orthodox Jews say that this is a command from God, whatever its original reason. Most Jews feel it is a tradition that keeps the Jews as separate, as special – this sets them apart as different – and so they do not want to stop these old customs, even though the original reasons for them no longer apply.

1 How many things have changed since Victorian times? Have a brainstorming session in groups.
2 Are all old laws irrelevant today?
3 Why do members of religions have arguments about their old rules?
4 What are the names for traditionalists and modernists among Jews?

▲ A choir in a Reform synagogue. Notice that there are men and women

One big difference between Reform and Orthodox Judaism is that men and women are treated differently. Three Jews explain some of the ways. The first two are Orthodox.

● (In the synagogue), the ladies are upstairs, the men are down here. The reason is that in Temple times it was already felt that it was not right for men and women to be praying together. It was feared that the men's attention might wander from the adoration of the Divine to the adoration of the women.

● We do have very different laws (for men and women) within the Orthodox religion. But it doesn't mean that we're not equal, just different. The men have more laws regarding the **community**, the women have more laws regarding the home.

● I found difficulties as a woman watching from the balcony at what was going on, and not feeling very involved. I find that in a Reform synagogue men and women do exactly the same, both in the actual synagogue service and in the governing of the community.

In this book you will find many ways in which Orthodox and Reform Jews are different. But remember that it is what Jews have in common which is most important. They share the belief in one God. They try to set a good example to others.

1 a) Why was Reform Judaism started?
   b) What do Reform and Orthodox Jews have in common?
2 a) In your own words, give an Orthodox reason for not changing the laws.
   b) Do you agree with it? Give reasons.
3 a) Why do you think the laws about women are mainly to do with the home?
   b) Do you think men and women should play equal parts in the synagogue and the community? Give reasons for and against.
4 a) Write down three ways in which girls and boys are expected to do different things at your school or in your home.
   b) What do you think is the reason for each difference?
   c) Do you agree with each reason? Say why.
5 a) Write a paragraph about three modern problems where it is difficult to decide what is right and what is wrong. Show that you understand why it is so difficult. (Some ideas to help you: nuclear weapons, unborn babies, drugs, pollution.)
   (b) How would (i) Orthodox and (ii) Reform Jews go about finding an answer to each problem?

Our clothes, badges and posters tell people a great deal about what matters to us – a poster supporting environmental issues may be displayed on a house; a football fan wears the strip and scarf. Human beings like to show how they feel through dressing up, or through decorating their homes. A house with a mezuzah nailed to the right-hand doorpost belongs to a Jewish family.

The Shema tells Jews that they should 'write them (words from the Shema) upon the doorposts of your houses and upon your gates'. In the early days, Jews engraved the words on the doorpost. Later, they found it was more practical to write on a scroll. They made a hole in the doorpost and put the scroll inside. For many hundreds of years, however, Jews have used a special case, like the one in the picture.

It contains a tiny parchment scroll, called a mezuzah, with the first part of the Shema written on it. The mezuzah shows visitors that it is a Jewish home. But its main purpose is to remind the family that God is always with them, so they should obey his commandments at all times.

Through the small window, you can see a Hebrew letter, the first letter in the Hebrew word for Almighty, one of the names given to God. Some Jews touch the mezuzah case when they enter or leave the house. This is a sign of respect for God's word.

▲ A mezuzah – a box containing part of the Torah

▲ This mezuzah is being fixed to a doorpost in Israel

The case in the picture on page 23 has a candlestick called a menorah. It reminds Jews of the one which used to be in the Temple in Jerusalem. Some mezuzah cases are made of gold or ivory. But a plain wooden or plastic one is just as good.

If a non-Jew were to place a symbol of something precious on their bedroom doorpost, what might it be? A photo of a boyfriend or girlfriend? A CD cover? This might seem an odd custom, but what ways do people have of displaying what is special to them?

● If we as Jews have survived as a people it is not because we have had mighty armies or great statesmen. It is because we've had **stable** homes and we grew up in places in which the feeling of happiness made up for many of the problems outside.

Lord Jakobovits

Jews feel that family life is very important, and they have many customs, such as touching the mezuzah, which helps the family celebrate together.

▲ *What is special to us?*

1 **a)** What is a mezuzah?

b) What does it remind Jews about?

c) Design your own mezuzah case. You don't have to have a menorah – your own patterns or other Jewish symbols will do.

2 Think what you might display on your doorpost instead of a mezuzah. What would be special for you, or your family? Draw a picture of this on a doorpost.

◄ *Inside a Jewish home*

Home is a special place. Perhaps you have looked forward to getting home to tell your family that your team has won a match, so they would know how pleased you feel. Or maybe you've had a row with your friends and wanted to tell someone at home all about it.

Home is where we learnt to talk, walk, feed ourselves, and play with toys. Those with brothers and sisters probably learnt how to fight and then make friends again. Our parents or guardians take care of us and teach us the things they feel we need to know.

It's the same in anybody's home. But what makes Jewish homes special is that Jewish parents want their children to follow the ways of Judaism. So the home is the place to learn what it means to be Jewish.

The Jewish father must:
• support his family
• study the Torah
• see that his children study the Torah.

The mother must:
• feed the family as the Torah instructs
• make sure her husband and sons have the right clothes

• prepare the home for the Sabbath and the festivals
• teach her daughters what they will need to know when they have their own homes.

Of course, in many families, especially in Reform homes, these jobs may be shared differently. But Orthodox mothers take their responsibilities very seriously. Karen and Sandy explain:

● Having children has made me more aware of my Judaism, because I have to make sure my children are aware of their **obligations**. I have to make sure my household is arranged to back up the instructions they receive in their religion school.

● The central point of the Jewish religion is the home. The home is where the children are brought up, where the education takes place. Where the **rituals** of Shabbat and the festivals take place.

And therefore, as the woman is called 'the **foundation** of the home', really I would say that the woman is the most important thing in Judaism.

25

1 Which of these words describe a Jewish mother's feelings about her place in the home? For each, explain your choice.
proud; not bothered; caring; worried; responsible; ashamed; important.

2 a) Write a paragraph on the part played by the mother in many Jewish homes.

  b) Why do you think Sandy calls the woman 'the most important thing in Judaism'?

  c) What do you think are the most important things *your* mother does?

  d) Do you think a man could do all these tasks just as well as a woman? Give reasons for your answers.

● Food

▲ *A kosher food counter in a top London store*

Everybody needs food and drink. Most people have some idea which things are good for them and which are not. We are guided by what doctors and other experts say, and, of course, by what we like or dislike. But there are so many things to choose from, it isn't always easy to decide.

Jews don't have quite such a problem. The Torah states clearly what they must not eat. It tells them how to kill the permitted animals as painlessly as possible. And it tells them they must soak meat before they cook it so that all the blood is removed.

It may seem strange that a religion tells its followers what they can eat, but Jewish people do not think so. Remember that they have promised to obey God's word in everything. Keeping the laws about food is one way of showing that they are doing this.

Reform Jews believe that some of the food laws are no longer necessary. But Orthodox Jews feel they are just as important today as when they were first given.

An important rule is that dishes with meat cannot be eaten at the same meal as ones with milk in them. Orthodox Jewish kitchens have separate pots and pans for cooking milk and meat recipes.

Children do not always understand the reasons for things they can and cannot do. One little boy asked what would happen if he ate a chocolate bar straight after his chicken. After all, he had seen his friends eating chocolate after meat and nothing happened to them.

His mother explained that nothing terrible would happen to him. It was just that, because they are Jewish, there are some things they do differently from other people.

Food which has been prepared according to the laws is called kosher food. It means 'fit' to eat. It is not always easy to buy kosher food, especially in country areas.

But Jewish families know that, by following the laws about food, they are helping to keep the special promise made to God. Eating together is important for family life. Following the food laws reminds Jews of their faith.

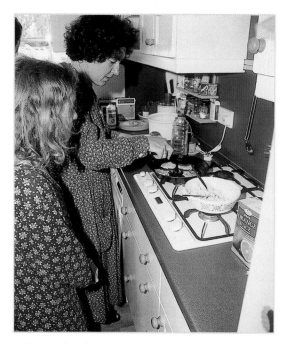

▲ *Preparing kosher food*

1 Read Deuteronomy 14: 3–21.

   a) Make two columns on a page. Head one column *yes* for permitted foods and the other *no* for foods which are not allowed. Then put these foods in the correct column:
   lamb chops; prawn-flavoured crisps; pork sausages; chicken curry and rice; cod and chips; ham and mushroom pizza; roast beef and Yorkshire pudding; ravioli on toast.

   b) In groups, plan a three-course meal for an Orthodox Jewish family. You may have as many vegetables and fruit as you wish.

   c) Compare your menus with the rest of your class and pick the best one.

   d) Are there any rules which govern the food you eat?

● Clothes

Most Jewish teenagers wear whatever they want to, or whatever their parents will buy for them! But for weekday morning prayers, Jewish men, and boys over thirteen, carry out some special instructions from the Torah.

The boy may have woken up thinking about the film he saw the night before, or the homework he forgot to do. But, while putting on his kippa, tallit and tefillin, he will have plenty of time to think about what they mean. So he is now ready to concentrate on his prayers.

Kippa – skull cap

My children wear their kippa whenever we're doing anything holy. Whenever we're having any of our ceremonies at home; whenever we're in synagogue; whenever it's a holy day; whenever they open a Holy Book.

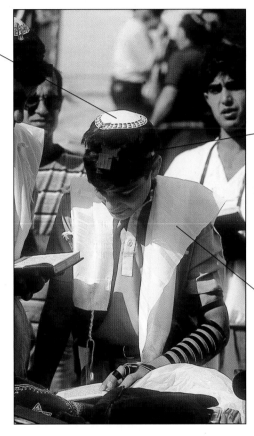

Tefillin – boxes containing words from the Shema

Tie them on your arms and wear them on your foreheads as a reminder.

Tallit – prayer shawl

Tell them to make fringes in the borders of their garments, so they may look upon them and remember all the commandments of the Lord.

Numbers 15: 38–39

---

1 a) Copy out this paragraph and fill in the missing words.

Jewish men may cover their _____ at certain times. Some wear a skullcap called a _____ all the time. Their tallit has _____ to remind them of God's _____ .

At some prayer times they also wear tefillin, one near the _____, the other near the heart.

b) Do you have clothes or other objects which you have to wear at certain times? Describe them and explain when and why you wear them.

c) Do you think it is a good idea to have to put on these special things? Give your reasons.

Food and rest are things that everyone needs to be healthy and contented. Everyone needs to eat, from the Queen to a child. Eating together is a valuable way of sharing time, and it is a great leveller. Everyone, old and young, rich and poor, come down to the same level if they share the same food.

If we work too hard and do not take time out to rest, then we can become bad tempered, stressed and ill. Taking regular times of recreation is important. Jews have a regular family meal together at the start of their weekly time of rest. The Hebrew word for rest is 'Shabbat', and this runs from Friday evening until Saturday night.

Jews cook whatever food they like, but there is always bread and wine. Special Shabbat loaves are bought, which are plaited. Jews must not work on Shabbat, but how do you define 'work'? Many rules and regulations have developed over the ages.

▲ *Relaxing on the beach*

▲ *Plaited loaves for the Sabbath and festivals*

1 Talk about a special meal that you have shared with others.
2 Can you recall one particular holiday or outing that you really enjoyed? Write a few lines about this, and use photographs, postcards or leaflets to illustrate it.
3 Write out a plan for a typical week, showing work times and recreation times. Mark on any regular activities (for example, music, sports) that you are involved in.
4 What food is always used at a Jewish Shabbat meal?

◀ *A Shabbat meal*

The word Sabbath means rest, but in many Jewish homes, and certainly in Orthodox ones, a great deal of hard work is done before the day begins.

The house must be clean and tidy, the Sabbath meal ready, the table laid with flowers and best plates and glasses, and the wine uncorked. Even the candlesticks have been specially polished. Everyone tries to do something to help.

And nobody forgets that this is a holy day. The Sabbath candles are lit as the Sabbath begins. Usually the mother does this. She recites a blessing as she does so. But in Sandy's home:

> ● The girls light their own candle, as their contribution towards **Shabbat.** It makes them an important part of the home. It's not just watching somebody else do something. They are involved.
>
>   Candlelight is different from electric light. It **signifies** peace coming into the house.

When the father and older boys come home from synagogue, the whole family wish each other 'Shabbat shalom' a happy Sabbath. The father blesses God, the Creator of the Sabbath. The blessing is usually made over wine, because it is a special occasion. This event is called Kiddush.

The father blesses the Sabbath, his children and two specially baked loaves called Challot. He also recites some verses from the Tenach. This is one way for a Jewish husband to thank his wife for everything she does.

After the meal, everyone thanks God for what they have enjoyed. An Orthodox Jewish girl explains why the Sabbath is important in her family.

> ● Our family looks forward to Shabbat because it is a time when we are all together. Our family get together on the Friday night and have a large meal.
>
>   We all enjoy this very much because we can talk about what has happened to us during the week; and we talk about the future and the past. The Sabbath is when the fast pace of the week slows down and we all relax and enjoy ourselves.

A drink of wine and blessings end Shabbat. A candle is lit and a spice box is brought out. Jews hope its sweetness will last for the next week.

1 Complete each of these sentences using the correct ending from the list on the right.

a)	Sabbath begins	in advance.
b)	Blessing God over wine	is on Friday.
c)	The main Sabbath meal	is called Kiddush.
d)	The meal must be cooked	at sunset on Friday.

2 a) Make a list of jobs which need to be done before the Sabbath begins.

b) Put a tick beside the ones which could be done by someone of your age.

No work on the Sabbath

Reform Jews are not strict, for example, they may drive to the synagogue

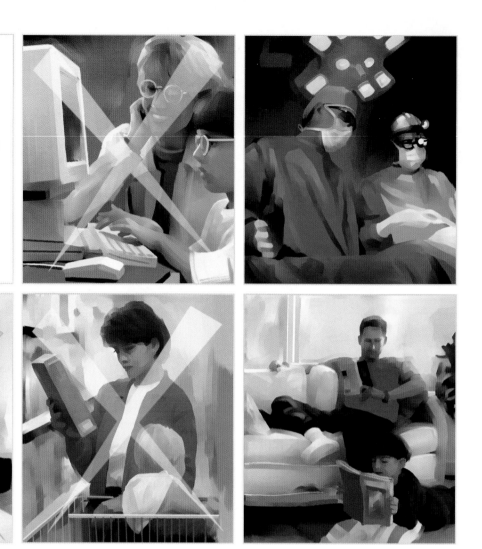

The fourth Commandment says, 'Remember the Sabbath Day, to keep it holy. In it thou shalt not do any work'. So the Sabbath is a special day for Jews.

Again, Herman Wouk describes his feelings. He has left the theatre in the middle of a rehearsal to get home for the beginning of the Sabbath.

● Leaving the gloomy theatre, the shouting stage-hands and the dense tobacco smoke, I have come home. It has been a startling change, very like a return from the wars.

My wife and my boys are waiting for me dressed in best clothes. We have sat down to a splendid dinner. My wife and I have caught up with our week's conversation. The boys, knowing that the Sabbath is the occasion for asking questions, have asked them. The Bible, the encyclopedia, the atlas, have piled up on the table.

Herman Wouk: *This is my God*

1 a) Read what Herman Wouk says about the Sabbath.
   b) Write down the words from this list which you think describe the Sabbath. For each one, explain your choice.
   happy; solemn; calm; relaxed; frantic; enjoyable; special; noisy; thoughtful.

2 Imagine you are a Jewish boy or girl. You need to finish some homework and you want to go shopping with a friend. A band is playing in the school hall on Friday evening. An aunt is sick in hospital and would like to see you. There is also a brilliant film on TV on Saturday night. How can you arrange your weekend if you have to keep the Shabbat?

● Naming and Circumcision

▲ *This boy is being blessed after his naming ceremony in a Reform synagogue*

A baby is born! For most families this is a marvellous reason for a celebration. Many cultures have some form of naming ceremony.

What's in a name? It is personal, part of you. It identifies you. It's more human and caring than being given a number. People are given names these days that their parents like. In the past, names were chosen very carefully, with a thought given to what they meant. In the Hebrew Bible, many names had special meanings, such as 'Micah' ('who is like God?') or 'Abraham' ('great father').

In Jewish families, the child is given at least one Hebrew and one ordinary name.

Karen, an Orthodox **Jewess**, explains her feelings when her babies were named.

> ● I felt part of an enormous family when my children were given their Hebrew names, and that I was carrying on a wonderful tradition. Our children were named in memory of our **deceased** relatives, so that they live on in our children.

Boy babies are circumcised, because God commanded Abraham:

> ● And he that is eight days old shall be circumcised among you, every male throughout the generations.
> *Genesis 17: 12*

31

▲ *The ceremony of circumcision, ending with a cup of wine over which Kiddush has been said*

Childhood

Children can go to special classes where they will learn about their religion. They often take place on a Sunday. Even children as young as three can go. The Talmud includes advice to teachers.

> ● Do not threaten a child; either punish him or forgive him.
>
> A classroom should never have more than 25 pupils.
>
> There are four categories of pupil: the sponge – he absorbs and retains everything; the funnel – everything that goes in comes out; the sifter – he remembers the trivial and forgets the significant; the sieve – he retains the important and sifts out the incidental.

▲ *Jewish children can attend special classes. They are taught about their religion and about important Jewish people, including Abraham and Moses*

Children are told about Abraham and Moses, as well as other people who have been important in the history of Judaism. They also learn to understand why Jews live and worship in the ways they do. Some lessons are spent learning to read and speak Hebrew.

This may be hard for some children, just as learning a foreign language may be difficult for them at secondary school. But, for most of them, it is worth it! One Jewish girl explains what it meant to her.

> ● I must have been about six or seven when I could read a little bit of Hebrew. I felt thrilled. I think being Jewish it is important to read Hebrew because God's book, the Torah, is written in Hebrew.

Letter	Pronunciation	Book Print
Aleph	Silent letter	א
Bet	b as in boy	בּ
	v as in vine	ב
Gimmel	g as in girl	ג
Dalet	d as in door	ד
Heh	h as in house	ה
Vav	v as in vine	ו
Zayin	z as in zebra	ז
Chet	ch as in Bach	ח
Tet	t as in tall	ט
Yod	y as in yes	י
Kaf	k as in kitty	כּ
	ch as in Bach	כ
Lamed	l as in look	ל
Mem	m as in mother	מ
Nun	n as in now	נ
Sameh	s as in sun	ס
Ayin	Silent letter	ע
Pey	p as in people	פּ
	f as in food	פ
Tsade	ts as in nuts	צ
Qof	k as in kitty	ק
Resh	r as in robin	ר
Shin	sh as in shape	שׁ
	s as in sin	שׂ
Tav	t as in tall	ת

▲ *The Hebrew alphabet. Jewish children learn to read Hebrew at an early age so they can read their holy book, the Torah, which is written in Hebrew*

Bat and Bar Mitzvah

Jewish boys and girls have a special birthday soon after they start secondary school. It is thirteen for a boy and twelve for a girl. A boy becomes Bar Mitzvah; a girl becomes Bat Mitzvah. It means Son (or Daughter) of the Commandments.

From now on it is their **responsibility** to carry out their duties to their family and their religion. Nobody is going to remind them!

It's a very special event, so most families hold a celebration. Relatives often come a long way; maybe from Israel or America. The whole family may attend a ceremony at the synagogue.

Boys read from the Torah for the first time. They spend a lot of time practising the part that they will read. In Reform synagogues girls also do this, but in most Orthodox communities it is still forbidden.

Now I have taken my Bar Mitzvah I can take part in synagogue services like the other men. I will wear the prayer shawl and the tefillin.

These strap two boxes to my forehead and left arm. They contain part of the Torah. The Law is to be in our minds and our hands.

▲ In a Reform synagogue, girls and boys read from the Torah when they become Bat or Bar Mitzvah

1 a) Draw this grid in your book and fill in the answers, using the clues below.

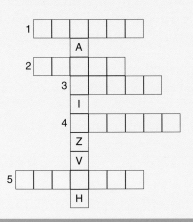

(i) The language of the Torah.
(ii) First five books of the Tenach.
(iii) He led the Exodus.
(iv) The study of the Torah.
(v) Father of the Jews.

b) Now, write the word which goes down. Why is this important to young Jews?

2 a) Write a paragraph describing how you think a Jewish boy feels when he becomes Bar Mitzvah.

b) Write a paragraph about a day in your life which was special. Explain why it was important and how you felt.

c) What sort of things help you to feel more grown up?

◄ *Happy ever after?*

A wedding is one of the happiest occasions in life. Most people would not marry unless they were in love with each other. But other things matter, too.

Sharing is one of the most important parts of marriage. People who have nothing, or very little, in common may have problems.

Being in love is not always plain sailing – your interests might conflict, such as someone who wants to go out all the time, and someone who wants to stay in and watch TV.

People who marry from different cultures and races have extra problems, but, if they really care for each other, it can work. It is not always easy, though, and Jews are strongly encouraged to marry other Jews. Orthodox Jews feel that they could not follow the Torah if they married a non-Jew.

Rosalind, an Orthodox Jewess explains:

> ● Religion as such is not so important in our marriage, but our **culture** and tradition is, regarding festivals and food, [for example].

She does not mean that religious beliefs do not matter. It's just that living with someone who had different ideas about everyday life would be difficult. So most British Jews do marry other Jews.

1 a) What difficulties might the couple in the photograph find?

b) Work out a role play about a girl who wants to marry someone of another race.

c) Is it important for a person to like all the same things that their marriage partner does?

2 Give two reasons why Jews usually marry other Jews.

34

▲ *The groom crushes a wine glass*

▲ *Under the huppah canopy*

At a Jewish wedding, the bride joins the groom under the huppah. This is a canopy on four poles which represents the couple's future home. It shows that the groom will look after his future bride.

The rabbi talks to the couple about their marriage. He blesses them, and they drink wine from the same goblet. This shows that they are going to share a life together. The groom places a ring on the bride's finger. He says in Hebrew 'Behold you are now married to me, with this ring, according to the Law of Moses and Israel.' She is now his wife.

The rabbi reads the Ketubah, the marriage agreement. It says that the groom has promised to take care of his wife.

The rabbi then recites seven blessings over the couple. He ends by praising God 'who has created joy and gladness, bridegroom and bride, love and brotherhood, pleasure and delight, peace and harmony.'

The final event may come as a surprise. The groom crushes a wine-glass on the floor with his heel! This is a reminder that the Temple in Jerusalem was destroyed many years ago. The newly-weds, too, will have to face bad times together as well as good.

The whole congregation shouts 'Mazel Tov!', which means 'Good Luck!'. The service is over. Everyone joins the newly-weds for a wedding party.

▲ *This Jewish graveyard is in Northern Ireland. Notice the Hebrew writing and the Star of David*

The last stage in the life cycle is death. Jewish burials take place as quickly as possible. Jews believe that rich and poor are equal after death, so the service is the same for everyone.

The coffin is plain and there are usually no flowers. Orthodox Jews are always buried, but Reform synagogues allow **cremation**. In Orthodox families, close relations make a small tear in their clothes to show their unhappiness.

The family of the dead person is expected to spend the next week at home. They are encouraged to talk about how they feel. Friends bring food for them, so they do not need to cook. The men do not shave and the women do not wear make-up. They may sit on low stools and wear slippers. This shows that their normal life has been interrupted by the death.

Every year, on the anniversary of the death of a parent, the children light a candle and say a special prayer called the Kaddish. But it does not mention the dead person. Instead, it praises God and asks for peace:

> ● Blessed, praised and glorified be the Name of the Holy One, blessed be He. He who makes peace in His high places, may He make peace for us and for all Israel, and say Amen.

1 a) What do close relations do after someone in a Jewish family dies?

b) Say what each of the following is a sign of: tearing the clothes; not shaving or wearing make-up; a plain coffin.

c) Do you think it is better to talk about something you feel very sad about, or to keep it to yourself? Give your reasons.

d) Why do you think the Kaddish praises God and does not mention the dead person?

2 Write a paragraph describing a wedding or a funeral you have been to. If it was not in a synagogue, point out which things were the same and which were different.

A minister in a synagogue is called a rabbi. It means 'my teacher'. The greater part of the rabbi's job is to teach his or her congregation to understand the Jewish way of life. Most rabbis are men but there are some Reform Jewish women rabbis.

● A REFORM RABBI DESCRIBES HIS WORK

● The rabbi's job is very largely teaching. You spend many hours teaching, both adults and children. But it goes further than that. You teach through your example. Your sermons should be teaching sermons. Your **conduct** is also a source of teaching.

You also have a responsibility for people's **welfare**. Making hospital calls is part of your duties. People who are sick are entitled to a visit from the rabbi. People who have got some difficulty should feel that the rabbi is available and can help.

Sometimes there may be a Jewish patient in hospital. [The nurses] are very concerned that they do the right thing when it comes to his or her diet. If it comes to his or her death, they may be very frightened of breaking laws. So you have got to give them instruction.

You are an **ambassador** to the outside world. It is important to go to schools to speak about Judaism.

The ritual of the community is your responsibility. If the wrong thing is done in a service it's your fault. You also have a [duty] to write articles, and to make announcements.

You should make sure that people in the community feel that they are useful. For example, most of the members of my staff are **volunteers**.

[What gives me special pleasure is] a job well done. For example, in the case of a funeral. If you feel that you've helped a family, that the whole thing has been done in the best possible way, that can give you a sense of satisfaction.

● AN ORTHODOX RABBI DESCRIBES HIS WORK

● My parish work is basically the same as any other minister. Visiting the sick, burying the dead, marrying those who wish to be married, seeing to the **spiritual** requirements that people have.

I go to the local jail and see the Jewish prisoners there. There is also a place for mentally retarded children. I go there and give them religious instruction.

If a person feels he or she has some problem that he or she wants to share, I certainly will listen to him or her. I can try to guide him or her along the right path, as far as is possible. Beyond that there is nothing that I can do that another person couldn't do equally well.

I am not God's policeman, it's not my job to chase people up. I myself try to keep everything very strictly and I like to think that my members do so too.

What makes me happy is when I see that a child who comes from a not very **observant** home is suddenly taking an interest in his or her religion and taking it seriously.

Taking the Torah scrolls out of the Ark ▶

A DAY IN THE LIFE OF A REFORM RABBI

TISHRI 22 5760   OCTOBER 15 1999

9.00
Make phone calls.

10.30
Appointment with authoress.

12.30
To cemetery - check lettering on headstone.

2.00
See Mr Barnet about conversion to Judaism.

3.00
Visit Mrs Morris in hospital.

4.30
Bar Mitzvah class.

6.30
Visit another synagogue.

10.00
Time for prayer.

1 a) Which of these words describe the kind of person a rabbi should be:
a good listener; thin; bad-tempered; kind; like a policeman; hard-working; a good example; thoughtful; impatient.
Give your reasons for each choice.

2 Pick out three people or groups of people a rabbi may see in his work. For each one, write a sentence explaining how he or she will try to help them.

3 a) Describe the rabbi's clothes.
b) Why do you think a rabbi wears white clothes for New Year?

4 Why do you think a person may become a rabbi? Try to think of at least two reasons.

5 In groups, make up an advertisement for a rabbi of a Reform synagogue. In your own words say what kind of person you are looking for. Compare your adverts with the rest of your class and decide which is the best.

6 You have thought about Jewish teachers (rabbis) in this chapter. Now think about your own teachers. What qualities do you think make a good teacher?

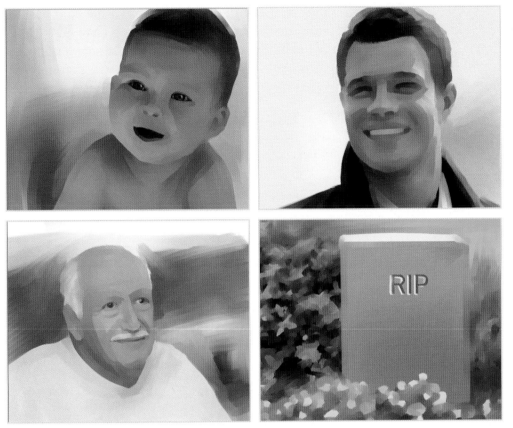

◀ *Seasons of life: the human cycle from birth to death*

Seeds are sown; the sun shines; the rain falls; the seeds sprout; the plants grow. This is the seasonal **cycle**. It happens every year. If the cycle is broken, people will not have enough food. From ancient times, different peoples have held special celebrations during the seasonal cycle, especially at spring time and harvest times to pray for blessing, and to give thanks. The long winter months might also have a festival of light, giving hope, and promising the spring to come.

The four seasons can be compared with the human life cycle, too, suggesting birth, growth into adulthood, old age and death.

Jews celebrate spring and harvest time with the festivals of Pesach and Sukkot. They also have a festival of light – Hanukkah – and a summer festival – Shavuot.

> ● Everything that happens in this world happens at the time God chooses. The time for planting and the time for pulling up.
>
> *Ecclesiastes 3: 1–2*

1 What might people want to pray for, or give thanks for, in each of the four seasons?
2 Create your own spring festival, using poems, music, drama and objects (flowers/seeds/water) to give thanks for the coming of new life in spring.
3 Design a CD cover showing the four stages of the human life cycle, and make up the titles of four songs, one for each season.

● Pesach – the Spring Festival

▲ *The Passover meal*

The evening is a mixture of sadness and joy. The Jews do not forget that they were once slaves. But they celebrate their freedom with a splendid meal, story-telling and singing. It means a late night for the children, but they look forward to it very much. In Karen's community they make sure that nobody is left out.

> ● We always have friends or relatives or people we don't even know to our **Seder** table. This is an occasion when we like to invite strangers, people who don't have anywhere to go, so that everybody has a Seder service to attend.

Spring-cleaning in a Jewish home means making the house ready for Passover. This is when Jews remember the Exodus.

There is a special meal and service at home. To make it easier to follow what happens, everyone has a book called the Hagadah. In this the Exodus story is often told in pictures, and the book also has hymns and songs.

Children take a special part in the Passover feast. The youngest asks, 'Why is this evening different from all other evenings?'

The oldest person in the family then reads the story of the Exodus, as Moses led the Hebrew slaves out of Egypt. The final plague to strike the land was the death of the firstborn, but the houses of the Hebrews were safe, passed over. Hence this festival is the Passover, or Pesach in Hebrew.

Karen describes part of the evening in an Orthodox family.

> ● We have a song which tells about all the things which God did for us at the coming out of Egypt. After each verse we sing 'Dayanu'. This means 'it would have been enough'.
>
> If he'd just taken us out, if he'd just opened the Red Sea, if he'd just given us food to eat, it would have been enough. At the end of each verse the children all shout out 'Dayanu!'

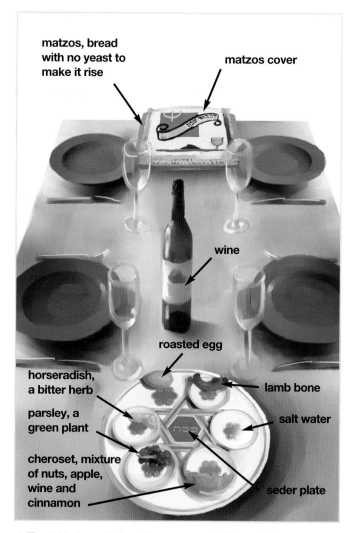

matzos, bread with no yeast to make it rise

matzos cover

wine

roasted egg

horseradish, a bitter herb

lamb bone

parsley, a green plant

salt water

cheroset, mixture of nuts, apple, wine and cinnamon

seder plate

▲ *The table is ready for a Passover meal. The egg and the lamb are not eaten. They are tokens. The lamb is a reminder of the meat eaten at the first Passover. The egg is a symbol of hope*

Shavuot

◄ *Children and adults celebrate the festival of Shavuot*

The summer months bring a celebration that gives thanks for the Torah. Jews believe that the Torah is there to teach and to guide, like a Highway Code through life. This festival remembers the time when Moses went up Mount Sinai and spoke with God. He was given the Ten Commandments, and later, other laws.

Every summer the Jews celebrate this event at the festival of Shavuot. The synagogues are decorated with flowers. The Jews thank God for these and for the Torah. Here is a special poem for Shavuot.

> ● Could we with ink the ocean fill,
> Were every blade of grass a **quill**,
> Were the world of **parchment** made,
> And every man a **scribe** by trade,
> To write the love of God above
> Would drain the ocean dry,
> Nor would the scroll contain the whole
> Though stretched from sky to sky.

Shavuot comes fifty days after Pesach, and was called 'Pentecost' in Greek (a name that survives as the Christian festival of the coming of the Holy Spirit, which took place at the time of Shavuot.) This festival adds responsibility to that of Pesach. The Jews were set free from slavery to serve the living God. They agreed to follow the Torah out of gratitude.

We all need guidance at times. Life can be confusing and hard. We sometimes need to work out what is the right thing to do. Friends, parents, youth leaders and writings by experts can help us. Jews believe that the Torah helps them to make many decisions about what is right and wrong.

41

1 a) Look at the picture of the Passover table.
b) Write each named item on a separate line and miss a line between each.
c) Next to it, copy out from the list below what each item is a reminder of. The first one is done for you.
roasted egg: Jews used to take an offering of food to the Temple.
the Jews left Egypt in a hurry – no time for bread to rise;
the slaves mixed cement for building;
salt tears of Jews in slavery;
bitter memories of hard times in Egypt;
lamb's blood was smeared on Hebrew doors;
Passover celebrates new life for Jews and all growing things;
a drop is spilt to remember the unhappiness caused by each plague.
d) Draw your own picture of the Seder table.
2 Imagine that you were to share your favourite foods and have a picnic in a special place. Write out a menu for this and describe the place.
3 Design a greetings card for Shavuot.

Sukkot – the Harvest Festival

The Jews who left Egypt with Moses did not have settled homes. They travelled for forty years in the desert. Their homes were **temporary** ones which they built to protect themselves from the weather, wild animals and enemies.

These shelters were called sukkot. They were not very strong. The Jews relied on God to protect them.

Jews today remember that God looked after their ancestors in the desert. Some modern Jews build sukkot in their gardens or help to build one in the synagogue. Karen describes the Sukkot celebrations in her family.

> We build a sukkah because the children love it and because it's another way for them to live the religion. Those of us who build sukkot, we have great parties, we have what's called a sukkah-crawl. We go from one sukkah to another and we drink wine and eat fruit. It's absolutely delightful.
>
> We eat in there and the children have their breakfast in there. But we don't sleep in there. However, in Israel, they do live in the sukkah.

Jews carry branches of palm, myrtle and willow, and citron fruit, during the festival of Sukkot. They wave them up and down to north, south, east and west. It shows that God is everywhere.

Simchat Torah

Simchat Torah comes at the end of Sukkot. It means 'Rejoicing of the Law'. The scrolls are carried around the synagogue seven times and all the congregation hold a big party.

▲ Dancing with the Torah

▲ A family celebration inside a Sukkot shelter

1 Why do some Jews build sukkot in their gardens or synagogues?

A Festival of Light – Hanukkah

▲ *Lighting the Hanukkah candle*

One of the first things they needed to do was relight the lamp in the Temple. There was only enough oil for one night and it would take eight days to get some more. They lit it anyway. But after one day, the lamp was still alight. It remained burning for eight days!

At Hanukkah, Jews have a special candlestick. It has places for eight candles as well as a servant candle which is used for lighting the rest. One candle is lit on the first evening, two on the second and so on.

It has become traditional to have parties and for children to be given presents. Schoolchildren sometimes put on Hanukkah plays.

---

1 Light is important in many religious and non-religious rituals.
  a) Why do you think this is so?
  b) Write down at least four occasions you know of when light is used for a special reason.

2 a) Why do you think it is important for Jews to remember Hanukkah?
  b) Write about a tradition your family keeps every year. It need not be connected with religion.

3 Draw a Hanukkah menorah and in the eight flames write about something that you hope for in life.

| nun | gimmel | heh | shin |

4 a) You need a piece of stiff card about five cm square divided into four sections. Write one of the Hebrew letters above on each section of the square.
  b) Make a small hole in the middle and push a used matchstick through it. You have a dreidel, a kind of spinning-top. Jewish children play games with them at Hanukkah.

5 Jews rejoice at Simchat Torah. A guide to life is important. In groups, put together an A5 booklet, 'A Highway Code to Life', using the headings 'Families'; 'Friends'; 'Boyfriends/girlfriends'; 'Fun'; 'The World'. Write down any ideas you have about these topics.

The winter months have a festival of light, Hanukkah, which speaks of hope and the presence of God. This falls about the same time as Christmas, and is greatly loved by Jewish children as they receive Hanukkah presents.

Hanukkah celebrates an event which happened two thousand years ago. The Syrian Greeks had conquered the Jews. They would not allow them to worship God. They put them to death if they read the Torah.

After years of fighting, a group of Jews managed to defeat the Greeks and drive them out of Jerusalem. They were free to worship again.

● Rosh Hashanah

> ● Whenever the Jews on Earth rejoice in their festivals, they give praise to the Lord. They put on fine clothes, and pile their tables with good food. So the angels ask, 'Why do the Jews pamper themselves so much?' And God answers, 'They have an important Guest today. I am with them.'
>
> *Writings of the Rabbis*

New Year is the time when Jews celebrate the creation of the world. They call it Rosh Hashanah. It comes on the first day of the Jewish month of Tishri, in September or October. The Jewish year 5761 began in 2000.

> ● These are days in which we look back and ask ourselves 'Have we really done what we were meant to do?' If we find **shortcomings** we should feel a sense of [guilt] and resolve 'Never again! Next year we'll be better'.
>
> Lord Jakobovits

There is a special New Year meal. The family dip their first piece of bread in honey and say, 'May God give me a sweet and happy New Year'. They have apples dipped in honey, too.

Jews believe that God keeps a Book of Life. It has the names of everyone who is sorry for doing wrong. Many families send Rosh Hashanah cards with the message 'May you be written in the Book of Life'.

God decides on the first day of the year who will be forgiven, but anyone who is left out has ten days to show he or she is truly sorry. During that time, Jews try to apologise to everybody they have been unkind to.

God makes his final judgement on Yom Kippur, which means Day of **Atonement**. Jews have a good meal the night before, because this is a day on which they do not eat or drink. Giving up something important is a sign that you are really sorry for doing wrong.

Synagogues are packed on Rosh Hashanah and Yom Kippur. They are called the High Holydays because they are the most important festivals in the Jewish year. Lord Jakobovits, who was the British Chief Rabbi, sent this message for Rosh Hashanah.

> ● I wish my fellow Jews and, through them, my fellow men, 'Shana Tovah', a good New Year. May we contribute to the wonderful world into which we were created.

▲ *The Shofar or ram's horn is sounded to call Jews to the synagogue during Rosh Hashanah. Why do you think a ram's horn is used?*

◄ Letting go of the past: confessions are burnt as people say 'sorry' to each other

45

Jews have the special ceremonies of Yom Kippur to say sorry and put things right before they start the new year. Many peoples have customs that try to start the new year afresh, with resolutions. It is a time to mark off, to reflect and to plan ahead.

People might need to put things right with each other, or God, at other times in the year. Some people, Jews or non-Jews, make up their own ceremonies to put the past behind them. A group who have hurt each other might spend time arguing, negotiating, saying sorry. This might happen with an agreed go-between, and they might choose to sit in a circle, with only one person being allowed to speak at a time. A ritual might follow this, such as writing out confessions of what they have done wrong, and then these are set alight in a metal container. Candles are lit from the flames, as signs of new life and hope.

Some schools have introduced circle time during the week, to discuss problems and share ideas.

1 a) Draw this grid in your book and fill in the answers, using the clues opposite. Note: some answers can be found in Chapter 12.

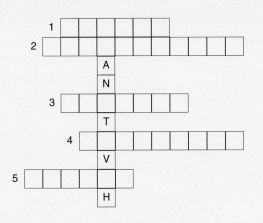

(1) Celebrates the Exodus.
(2) Jewish New Year.
(3) Celebrates the giving of the Law.
(4) Day of Atonement.
(5) Ram's horn.

b) Now, write the words which go down and explain what they mean.

2 a) Design a ceremony of forgiveness. First of all decide which people or groups are going to be involved. What might they do to say sorry? Would special, appropriate gifts be given?

b) What is the difference between atonement and just saying you are sorry?

c) Do you think it is a good idea to try to remember things you have done wrong? Give your reasons.

● Purim

There is another time when Jewish children dress up and act out a story. It is called Purim and falls in February or March.

It's a time when Jews remember Esther. Esther was Queen of Persia. She was also Jewish, but her husband did not know this. The King's chief minister was Haman. He hated the Jews.

Esther's uncle would not bow down to Haman. Haman was so angry that he plotted to have all the Jews killed, and he **drew lots** to decide on the date. The Persian word for lots was Purim.

Anyone who went to see the King without permission was put to death. But Esther dared to go and tell her husband of Haman's wickedness. The King forgave her for breaking the law and Haman was put to death.

The full story is in the Book of Esther in the Bible. It is read out in the synagogue. Every time Haman's name is mentioned, the children stamp their feet, boo and hiss and shake rattles. They're trying to drown out Haman's name. It is rather like a pantomime, where everyone boos the villain.

After the synagogue service, some children put on fancy dress and visit Jewish houses. They collect money for charity. They may sing:

> ● Today is Purim, tomorrow no more.
> Give me a penny.
> I'll be gone from your door.

▲ These cakes are called Haman's Ears! When do you think they are eaten?

▲ All dressed up for Purim

1 Why do you think it is important for Jews to remember Purim each year?

2 Draw a series of pictures to tell the story of Esther.

3 Read part of the Book of Esther out loud in class, such as Esther 3: 1–6. Have people cheer when Mordecai is mentioned, and boo when Haman is mentioned.

4 In your books, design a fancy dress costume for a Purim celebration.

5 Can you think of a situation today where a person might be threatened because of their race or religion?

Young People and Judaism

14

- The world exists only through the breath of schoolchildren.

  The Talmud

▲ *Jewish young people on their way to school*

The Talmud makes a striking claim – the world exists only through the breath of schoolchildren. Young people are the future.

If people stopped having children the human race would die out. Of course, that is not very likely. But if people stopped learning how to make computers or play tennis those skills would die out, and it would not be easy to start them off again.

Young people need to learn many skills from the past **generations**, but we must expect that they will have new ideas, too. This is especially true in a highly technological society, with new inventions and styles of communication. There will be new ideas about fashion, music and recreation too. Youth involves the tension of learning the best of the old, and being open to the future. If everything that has gone before is written off as 'old', then we would make many mistakes, and lose good ideas. If we think only of what is 'new' then we are never settled, always moving on.

In the past, before we had so many new inventions, older people were the wise ones, and they were treated with great respect by society. Today, it is very easy for them to feel left behind, bewildered by change.

Young Jews are taught many customs and religious rules, such as what foods not to eat, and what to wear at certain times. This might cause problems for some, but others want to keep their identity, and do not mind being different from their friends, sometimes.

47

1 a) In groups, make a list of all the ideas and skills that you have been taught by parents or other adults.

b) Strike out any of the above items that you do not think are important today.

c) What would you like to change about your way of life?

d) Feed back in groups to the rest of the class.

2 a) What tensions might young Jews feel between the past and the present?

b) What reasons do many young Jews have for keeping the old traditions?

If Jewish children did not learn about Judaism from their parents and teachers, then their religion and way of life would come to an end. The reason there are still Jews today, thousands of years after Abraham, is that adults have shown their children how to follow the Jewish faith.

The Torah instructs parents to instruct their children. The wearing of the Tefillin is a reminder of this. The Law is to be kept in the head and the heart – in memory and practice. The keeping of festivals such as Pesach, or of the weekly Shabbat, teaches the whole family.

Karen and Rosalind belong to Orthodox communities. Their children are aged between three and twelve. One of Karen's favourite verses in the Torah is, 'You shall teach them (the commandments) to your children'. Rosalind gave this reason for wanting her children to learn about Judaism.

> ● The children must be educated to understand their culture, traditions and religion. Then they can at least choose with knowledge. They can marry Jews or not, be Orthodox or not, [knowing] what they are taking on.

Jewish children learn a lot at home, but they can also go to religion school. Some young people go until they are nineteen. They take Jewish Studies and can train as teachers. They help with the younger classes, telling Bible stories and teaching the Hebrew alphabet.

But it's not all hard work! There are Jewish youth clubs, too. They often organise camps so that young people can meet Jews from outside their neighbourhoods. This is what one teenage girl wrote about the camps she has attended.

> ● The camps are incredible fun. At the camps there are themes throughout the week. Themes that have been used at camp are Israel, Kibbutz, Jews around the world, and learning about the **Holocaust**. I have been attending the camps since I was seven and every year I enjoy them more and more.

Her youth group also goes to camps in Israel. One of the aims of the camps is to persuade young Jews to live in Israel. The summer camps give them a chance to find out what it is like.

1 a) Write a sentence to describe how Jewish children learn about Judaism.
   b) Why is it important that they do this? Give at least two reasons.
   c) What is Rosalind's reason?
   d) Do you think it is a good one? Explain your answer.
2 a) Which of these words do you think describe the Jewish camps? Give a reason for each choice.
   fun; boring; friendly; interesting; expensive; dangerous; happy.
   b) Where else can young Jews meet each other?
   c) Where do you meet young people who have the same interests as you?
   d) Write a paragraph describing one of your interests.

▲ *Children of all ages enjoy life at camp*

There have been Jewish communities in Britain for over three hundred years. Now there are more than 300 000 Jewish people here. Most of them live in London or other big cities. This is what three Jewesses feel about being Jewish in a non-Jewish country.

- I think many communities, particularly outside large cities, are similar to ours. We all (except two families) drive and use electricity on Saturday. We send our children to English state schools, eat non-kosher meat and bread and drink non-kosher milk.

  And yet we remain a community. We have social gatherings and festival services, celebrations and parties.

- As a Jew I have found no problems. Many Jews are well-**integrated** into non-Jewish society while able to retain their Jewishness. Many [of us] talk to groups and individuals about Judaism and invite friends to share in Jewish festivals and services.

- Practical difficulties are the problems about buying kosher food in **rural** areas. Also most shops are open on Saturdays (our Sabbath) and closed on Sundays (our weekday).

  Children must make their own way as individuals who are different in school from as early as the age of five. This can be [upsetting], especially at Christmas time.

Most Jews mix freely with non-Jews at work or school or in their neighbourhood. This does not mean that they feel less strongly about their Judaism, as this Orthodox teenager explains.

- I do not think that being Jewish affects my friendships because most of my friends are non-Jewish. But I would not get into a serious relationship with a non-Jewish boy and I shall definitely marry a Jew.

▶ A kosher restaurant in London

Members of Karen's synagogue volunteer to help both Jews and non-Jews.

● We support a local Jewish mentally handicapped home. Many of our community are
'aunties and uncles' there. They take the children home for tea, or they take them out
for the afternoon.
    We operate trolleys and the visitors' shop at the local hospital. But that's not just
the Jewish community. It's organised by the Red Cross and we have a day for doing it.

▲ *Returning from Yom Kippur prayers at a synagogue in London*

The Council of Christians and Jews was founded
in Britain in 1942. Its main aim is for Christians
and Jews to understand each other's religions. It
hopes to make sure that, in future, people will not
be **prejudiced** against members of different
religions. Madeleine's experience suggests that this
is happening.

● I personally have felt in recent years a desire among
sections of the non-Jewish community to learn about
and understand the Jewish religion. Many in my
community feel strongly about understanding other
minorities and being understood.

The Archbishop of Canterbury called for
Christians and Jews to act together. This was his
reason:

● The shared belief in One God is a **summons** to us to
speak again and again together to the modern world.

1 a) What problems do Jewish rules create for adult
Jews in Britain?
b) How do some Jews help other people to
understand Judaism?
c) What problems may there be for Jewish children?
d) How do you think non-Jewish children can help
them?

2 If you are Jewish, perhaps your teacher will arrange for
you to tell the class about some aspect of Judaism in
Britain which interests you.

● Lord Immanuel Jakobovits

About three thousand mourners paid their respects to a former chief Rabbi, Lord Immanuel Jakobovits, in October 1999. Lord Jakobovits was a chief Rabbi of Jews in the UK from 1967 to 1991, who died aged 78.

He had come to Britain from Germany, escaping persecution by the Nazis in the 1930s. He found a warm welcome in this country, and was taken into the confidence of many political and religious leaders. He was a personal friend of Margaret Thatcher when she was Prime Minister in the 1980s and Tony Blair, the Prime Minister at the time of his death, sent this message:

> ● Lord Jakobovits was a man deeply respected and widely admired through the whole of this country for his faith, his ability and his courage.

Lord Jakobovits did a great deal to help relationships between British Reform and Orthodox Jews. An Orthodox Jew himself, he held secret talks between the different groups who tended to be very suspicious of each other. Having survived the Nazis, he was determined to unite Jews wherever he could.

Here was a refugee Jewish boy who had been taken to the heart of British society, and honoured by being given a seat in the House of Lords. He also worked hard to improve relations between Christians and Jews.

▲ *Lord Jakobovits*

1 Why was Lord Jakobovits admired by two Prime Ministers of this country?

2 Why do you think it was so important for Lord Jakobovits to work for peace and understanding between different Jewish groups?

3 Imagine you were Lord Jakobovits, aged thirteen, arriving in this country. Describe how you might have felt.

● So long as you can feel
the cold –
the wet –
the hunger,
and the lice –
which itch,
and drink your blood
You are alive –
Rejoice
You will survive
Be strong,
it can't be long.

Michael Etkind, a survivor of the Holocaust

▲ *Praying at the Western Wall. Note the prayers written on the papers in the holes in the wall*

In 70CE (Common Era), the Romans attacked the Holy City of Jerusalem, the centre of the Promised Land. They destroyed the Temple. Hundreds of thousands of Jews were killed and many carried off to Rome as slaves.

● It's hard to understand what the loss of Jerusalem, and especially the Temple, meant to those Jews of old. It was so much more than just blocks of stone to them.

   To begin with, they believed with all their hearts that the '**divine** presence' inhabited the Temple. They believed that when it was destroyed by the Romans, this presence left it – and where was it then to be found?

Lynne Reid Banks: *Letters to my Israeli Sons*

The Temple has never been rebuilt. All that remains of it is the Western Wall that holds up the mount on which the Temple stood. This is popularly known as the Wailing Wall, as Jews go there, even today, to **lament** the destruction of the Temple. After its destruction, the Jews were scattered in countries all over the Middle East and Europe. This scattering is called the Diaspora.

Many people hated the Jews or were afraid of them. This may have been because the Jews were different from them in some ways.

▲ *Jews in the Middle Ages sometimes had to wear special clothes to make them look different*

Hatred of Jews is called anti-Semitism. One of the most terrible examples of this took place in Europe before and during the Second World War. Hitler, the leader of Germany, thought that Jews were sub-human and wanted to destroy them all.

Anne Frank was a Jewish teenager living in Amsterdam. For nearly three years she kept a diary. The early sections are like those of any teenage girl today. She describes her classmates, girls and boys, such as:

> ● J.R. – I could write a whole book about her. J. is a detestable, sneaky, stuck-up, two-faced gossip who thinks she's so grown up. She really got Jacque under her spell, and that's a shame. J. is easily offended, bursts into tears at the slightest thing, and, to top it all, is a terrible show-off. Miss J. always has to be right ...

Later, when the Germans occupied Holland in 1940, new laws were introduced that made life very difficult for the Jews.

> ● Jews must wear a yellow star, Jews must hand in their bicycles, Jews are banned from trams and are forbidden to drive. Jews are forbidden to visit theatres, cinemas, and other places of entertainment. Swimming baths, tennis courts and other sports grounds are all prohibited to them. Jews may not visit Christians.

In 1942, the Nazis began rounding up Jews in Germany and **occupied** countries in Europe. For two years, Anne and her family lived in hiding in Amsterdam. In all that time she did not give up hope.

> ● In spite of everything I still believe that people are really good at heart. If I look up into the heavens, I think that it will all come right. Peace will return again.

Anne was taken to a concentration camp when her family was discovered, and she survived until 1945, dying from disease only about a month before the camp was liberated by the British on 12 April 1945. She was fifteen. Her father, Otto, was the only member of the family to survive after the war, and he kept his daughter's diary. This was published and became a best seller.

▲ *Anne Frank*

The Nazis took the Jews to **concentration camps**. The strongest had to work like slaves. Many died from disease or starvation. The majority were gassed or shot, and burned. The Nazis caused the deaths of twelve million people. Nearly half of them were Jews. This mass-murder is called the Holocaust.

At Dachau, in Germany, one of the concentration camps is now a museum. On the wall is written, in French, English, German and Russian, the words:

NEVER AGAIN

Many people, not only Jews, are determined that young people will learn about what happened. They hope that this will prevent anything like it happening again.

Karen is an Orthodox Jewess who goes into schools to talk about Judaism.

> ● Perhaps one day one of those children that I speak to might meet someone who doesn't do things quite the way they do things. Who maybe won't eat the same food as they eat; who maybe has their head covered.
>
> And perhaps they will understand why, and they will **tolerate** it. And it just might make the world a little easier to live in.

◀ Remembering the dead . . . a Jewish ceremony at the entrance to a Polish concentration camp in 1995

1 Which of these words describe Michael Etkind or Anne Frank or both? Give a reason for each choice.
hopeful; greedy; brave; strong; desperate; trusting; unkind; stupid; afraid; patient.

2 a) Using your own words, write a paragraph on what life was like for Jews in a country occupied by the Germans.
   b) Draw a picture strip to show four things Jews were not allowed to do.

3 Write a sentence describing how you think the Jews felt when their Temple was destroyed.

4 a) Why do you think we should remember the Holocaust?
   b) Suggest at least two ways in which we can make sure people remember.

> ● Next year in Jerusalem.
>
> Seder Service

Thousands of Jews lost their homes during the Second World War. Afterwards, many countries agreed that Jews should have a land of their own; the land which God promised to them at the time of Abraham. So the State of Israel was set up in 1948. Amiram was nine years old at the time.

> ● It was during the night. We were asleep and everybody was listening to the only radio in the **kibbutz**. When the news came they woke us up and brought us to the dining-hall. Everybody was dancing. We were in our pyjamas and on our parents' shoulders.

Not everyone accepted the State of Israel. Arabs had lived in **Palestine** for two thousand years. They did not want to hand part of their land over to the Jews. Since 1948 there have been a number of wars between Israel and her Arab neighbours.

In the Six-Day War of June 1967, the Israelis captured the part of Jerusalem which had been in Arab hands since 1948. The importance of this success was summed up by Michael Elkins.

> ● And so it was that on the morning of June 7 1967, going with the paratroopers, I stood for the first time at the (Western) Wall. At Judaism's most sacred shrine. And I, who am not an observant Jew, covered my head and wept. As all the ancestors back through all the generations of Jews that link me to Abraham would have done.

55

STAR OF DAVID

STRIPES OF TALLIT

▲ *The modern city of Jerusalem*

◀ *The Israeli flag. David was the King who made Jerusalem the centre of Israel three thousand years ago*

◄ Yitzhak Rabin (left) and Yasser Arafat (right) shake hands to seal the 1993 peace agreement as President Clinton looks on

The problem of the land of Israel is still not solved. Some Arabs and Jews still fight each other. The photograph above shows the head of the Palestinian Liberation Organisation, Yasser Arafat, shaking hands with the then Prime Minister of Israel, Yitzhak Rabin. The two leaders agreed to work for peace. Sadly, a Jewish **extremist** shot dead Mr Rabin not long after this, and the leaders are still struggling to maintain the peace process.

Much hard feeling, and years of bloodshed, lie behind this struggle. Neither side has clean hands, and they have hurt each other. Both sides have bombed, gunned people down, or fired missiles. Memories go back a long way. Jews and Arabs have been cruel to each other.

► Jews and Palestinians **campaign** side-by-side for peace

Among Jews, there are different points of view about the land of Israel.

- Israel was given by God to the Jewish people. I believe in the biblical **boundaries** of the State of Israel.

  Malvyn Benjamin, Orthodox

- I agree that Israel is a God-given land. But my religious beliefs do not include an idea of boundaries as being more important than peace.

  Charles Emmanuel, Reform

The Jews will not give up the land God promised them. They will continue to try to reach agreement with all their Arab neighbours. Then their Promised Land will be at peace.

- The State of Israel is so very important because it is the true home of the Jews. Being Jewish is not just a religion. It is also a nationality.

  I think that after all our forefathers have been through to keep our homeland, everyone should make aliyah there. I feel strongly about returning to Israel, so strongly that I am returning once I am eighteen.

  Orthodox girl

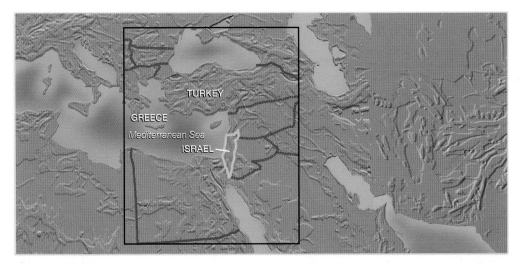

▲ *The Middle East today*

1 a) Copy the flag of Israel.
  b) Why do you think it has the Star of David and the lines on it?
2 a) Copy the map of the Middle East into your book.
  b) Using an atlas, name the Arab countries which border Israel. How many are there?
  c) Why did the Arabs object to the setting-up of the State of Israel?
  d) Do you think it was right for the Jews to be given land where Arabs had lived for many years? Try to give reasons for and against.

3 a) Why do you think it is not easy for Jews and Arabs to live in peace today?
  b) Design a peace protest banner.
  c) Devise a symbolic act of forgiveness and friendship that the leaders of the Arabs and the Jews could use.
4 Read all the quotations.
  a) Write down the names of each person.
  b) Write a sentence for each, describing what you think are their feelings about Israel.

There are about fourteen million Jews today. They live in many different countries. Nearly a quarter live in Israel. Many Jews live in the USA. New York alone has a Jewish population of just under two million.

Jews have been affected by the countries they live in and the people they have met. Their beliefs have not changed, but some of their traditions may be different.

In most countries, Jews are free to live as they wish. They can meet in synagogues, hold festivals and study the Torah without being afraid.

However, this is not true everywhere. In the old days of the Soviet Union, for example, life was difficult for Jewish people. Many synagogues were closed. But many Jews kept their beliefs and lived the Jewish way of life as far as they could.

One problem was that the government would only allow a very small number of Jewish books to be published. So, when there was an Israeli stand at the 1987 Moscow Book Fair, Jews from all over the Soviet Union went there.

They went to see the books about Israel and Judaism on display. It was also a chance to talk to other Russian Jews and to the Jews who had come from Israel to show the books. Read what one Israeli said.

> ● I will never forget a fourteen-year-old boy who had travelled a thousand miles by train to get to the fair. He had queued for five hours and then had less than an hour to look at the books and talk to the Israelis before setting off on his return journey – clutching a Magen (Star of) David we gave him.

Many Russian Jews would like to live in Israel or America. They have to ask for permission to leave Russia. At first the government may refuse, so these Jews are known as refuseniks. One man waited twenty years before he was allowed to leave.

People in other countries used to write letters or hold **demonstrations** to persuade the Soviet Union to allow more Jews to leave. Now that the Union has broken up into Russia and other smaller areas, such as Latvia, Jews have more freedom. Anti-Semitism is still around, though.

▶ *Saying prayers in a synagogue in North Africa*

Ida Nudel was a refusenik for sixteen years. Her sister Elana Friedman wanted her to be able to join her in Israel.

There is a happy ending to her story. Ida was finally given permission to go to Israel. She had this message for her supporters.

> ● I thank people of goodwill the world over, from Presidents and Prime Ministers to people from all walks of life. I want to thank all of you who campaigned for me.
>
> Never feel that your struggle is in vain. All those years, I felt the sympathy from thousands of people, Jews and non-Jews alike. You must continue the struggle.

Some Jews in Russia were imprisoned for criticising the government. Nathan Sharansky was in jail for nine years. During his time in prison, he was given a book of the Psalms by his wife.

> ● Through this I felt my connection with my wife, with my people, my history, with God. It helped me to feel myself together with my wife and with my people during all those years. I started strikes. I refused to work. In that year I spent 186 days in the punishment cell. But finally they returned the Psalm book to me.

▼ *These Jews hope that they will soon be reunited with their friends and relatives*

1 a) Think of at least two ways in which people's lives might change when they go to live in another country.
  b) How might life be difficult for them if they did not change?
  c) Write down at least two ways in which you and your family could help a family from another country who moved to live next door.
  d) Write down any reasons you can think of why strangers may not seem to want your help.

2 a) For each of the following, write a sentence to say what they did to get something they really wanted: the Jewish teenager; Elana Friedman; Nathan Sharansky.
  b) Who do you think had the most difficult task? Give reasons.

3 Design a poster about allowing Jews freedom of worship or movement.

> ● The Law of Moses has changed them that come into contact with it, even though they seem to have cast the Law aside.
>
> Yehuda Halevi, twelfth-century Jewish poet

The way you talk and dress and eat and think can all be affected by other people. For example, you speak English because most people in this country do.

Judaism has influenced many people's lives. If you are a Muslim or a Christian you may have spotted that Judaism has some things in common with your religion. The most important is that they share the belief in one God. But there are other links.

The Tenach is the Old Testament of the Christian Bible. You may have heard the stories of Noah's Ark, Jonah and the Whale, and Daniel in the Lions' Den. These are all tales from Jewish Holy Books. Some of the characters in the Muslim holy book, the Qu'ran, and in the Tenach are the same people too.

The Ten Commandments are as important to Christians as to Jews. There is a reading from the Old Testament in church services, and Christians sing Psalms, written by the Jewish King David.

There is a good reason why so many things are the same. All three religions can trace their beginnings back to Abraham.

Jesus Christ, the key figure of Christianity, was a Jew. He was descended from Abraham and his son, Isaac. Muhammad, the key figure of Islam, was an Arab. He was descended from Abraham and his other son, Ishmael.

Flora Solomon lives in a flat in London. She is Jewish. Many of her neighbours are Arabs.

> ● I met one in the lift the other day and I said, 'I am a Jew and you are an Arab so we should be safe from any bombs'. And he said 'Madame, we are cousins,' and he kissed my hand!

Rabbi Gershon Cohen sums up two important effects of Judaism.

> ● Everybody knows that a week is seven days. The Lord rested from His creation on the seventh day. No other people had that [idea] of having a seven-day week. That's one of the [gifts of Judaism] to the world at large.
>
> [Another practice that grew up as a result of Judaism is the law of] charity to the poor. You may not neglect any suffering. Let me take one example that made a deep impression upon me as a child. If you see your neighbour's horse or donkey lying collapsed in the street, you may not ignore it. You must help that beast and your neighbour.

Rabbi Julia Neuberger sums up what she thinks is Judaism's main message to its followers and to the world.

> ● I think there is a duty upon you to do God's will. To me, a lot of it is being concerned for the wider community, being concerned for the **oppressed,** the prisoners, looking to the poor. It seems to me that that's the great message of Judaism.

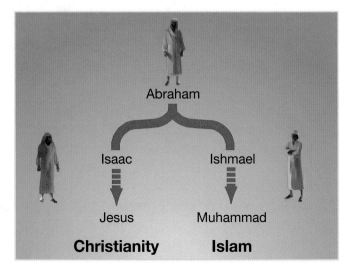

▲ Abraham's family tree

Jews, Christians and Muslims share many beliefs. They all worship the one God. Christian Holy Communion derives from the Jewish custom of using bread and wine at sacred meals. Sadly, the three faiths, though spiritual cousins, do not always live in peace. They have fought and persecuted each other. Today, many people are trying to encourage others to live in peace, and to learn from each other. There is so much in common. If great religions cannot live in peace, how can the nations of the world?

Yad Vashem is a memorial to all the Jews killed in the Second World War, where flames burn day and night. Racism is a great evil. Races, faiths and cultures can be very different, but need not threaten anyone else. The Jews, along with others, remind us that all have rights, and all have their own, special ways.

◄ This statue at Yad Vashem shows the pain Jews felt as victims of racism during the Second World War. How does this make you feel?

1 a) Copy Abraham's family tree.

   b) Explain how Judaism, Islam and Christianity are linked.

   c) Give examples of at least two things which are the same or similar in Judaism and one other religion.

2 a) What is Yad Vashem?

   b) Design a memorial sculpture, flame or plaque to remember all who have suffered from racism.

   c) Draw two cartoons of two ordinary people. Have one saying a reason why he or she is racist, and have the other saying why racism is wrong.

3 Which do you think is the most important gift Judaism has given to the world? Give reasons.

Glossary

aliyah – to return to Israel and to make your home there
ambassador – someone who represents another country
Atonement – coming back to God after doing wrong

bimah – raised platform in a synagogue
boundaries – dividing lines between countries

campaigned – did things for a particular reason
circumcised – had loose skin of penis cut off
commandment – order (from God)
community – group of people
concentration camp – place in which people are forced to stay
conduct – behaviour
congregation – group of people who worship together
creation – everything that was made
cremation – burning
culture – development
cycle – complete set of events

deceased – dead
demonstrations – protest marches
descendants – members of family who are born after
divine – of God
drew lots – decided by picking from a bag of small objects

extremist – someone with extreme views

famine – lack of food
foe – enemy
foundation – what everything else depends on

generation – people born about the same time

headstone – gravestone
holocaust – total destruction

integrated – mixed with

Jewess – female Jew

Kiddush – blessing said over wine
kippa – prayer cap

lament – show sorrow for
liberation – freedom
logo – sign

minorities – small groups of people

negate – say it doesn't exist

obligation – what you have a duty to do
observant – obeying the Law
occupied – taken over by force
oppressed – kept down by force

Palestine – ancient home of the Jews
parchment – animal skin prepared for writing on
plague – a disaster that strikes an area
prejudiced – having an opinion without a good reason
progressive – modern and forward thinking

quill – kind of pen

responsibility – what you must do
ritual – to do with religious occasions
rural – country

sacrifice – making an offering to God
scribe – writer
Seder – Passover service at home
sermon – speech by minister
Shabbat – Sabbath
shortcomings – failures
Siddur – Jewish prayer-book
signifies – stands for
spiritual – to do with religious things
stable – firm
summons – call
synagogue – Jewish place of meeting

tallit – a prayer shawl
tefillin – straps and boxes containing part of the Torah
tolerate – allow without interfering
typhoon – violent storm

universe – everything which exists

volunteers – people who do things without pay

welfare – well-being
worship – show respect for God

Index